The FIRST BOOK of
THE OCEAN

The FIRST BOOK of
THE OCEAN

by Sam and Beryl Epstein

Pictures by Walter Buehr

FRANKLIN WATTS, INC.
575 LEXINGTON AVENUE · NEW YORK 22

SECOND PRINTING

Library of Congress Catalog Card Number: 60-11173

© Copyright 1961 Franklin Watts, Inc.

Printed in the United States of America
by Polygraphic Company of America

Contents

The World's Ocean

MANY maps of the world show that there are five oceans — the Atlantic, the Pacific, the Indian, the Arctic, and the Antarctic.

6

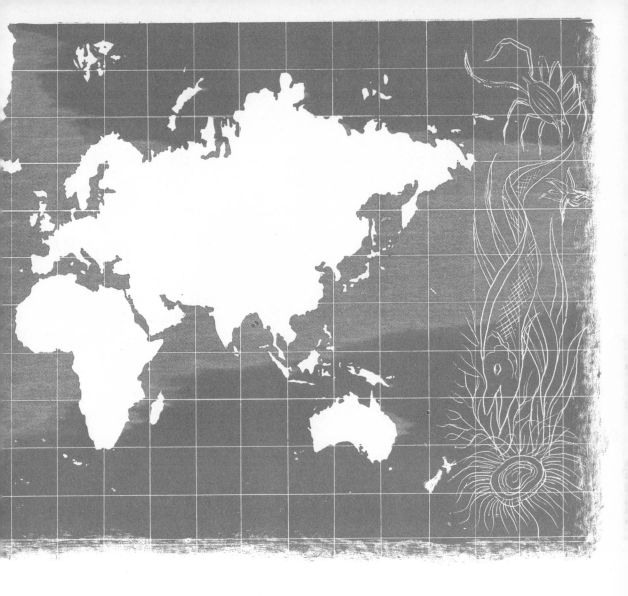

Other maps show only four. On those maps the word Antarctic doesn't appear.

But ask an *oceanographer* how many oceans there are, and this expert in ocean geography will say there is only one. He will say

7

that all the oceans shown on maps, along with dozens of seas and gulfs and bays, are really parts of a single body of water — the one vast ocean of the earth.

Some of the shores of this ocean are always solid ice. Some are smooth white stretches of tropical sand. Still others are craggy rocks or steep cliffs of stone or clay. And the waters of the ocean constantly move around and around the earth, from one of those shores to another. The drop of water that is whipped into foam today against the rocky coast of Maine, may touch a Pacific coral reef some months or years from now.

The continents of the earth — North and South America, Europe and Asia, Africa and Australia — are really only islands in this great body of water. And the ocean is much larger than all the continents put together. The world's mighty ocean covers almost three-fourths of our earth's surface.

8

A Walk Along a Beach

THERE are many mysteries of the ocean that have not yet been explained, even by experts who spend their lives studying the sea. But you can learn a great deal about the sea in a single summer afternoon, just by taking a walk along a beach.

Even before you reach the strip of sand edging the water, you will know that the sea is salty because you will smell the salt in the air.

You will also feel coolness against your skin before the ocean even comes into sight. This tells you that in summer the ocean is cooler than the land around it.

Then, as soon as you reach the beach, you will see a dozen things at once, and each one will tell you something about the ocean.

9

You see people in bathing suits splashing about in the waves, and others riding surfboards. You see a boy walking into the sea in a skin-diving mask, and a fisherman in hip boots casting his line into the surf. They all tell you that the ocean is one of the world's most popular playgrounds.

A trawler, dragging its nets half a mile offshore, tells you that fishing in the sea is a business as well as a sport, and that the ocean is one of the world's most important sources of food.

The gulls circling around the trawler, waiting for a chance to snatch at the fish in the nets, tell you that birds too find food in the sea.

Far out beyond the little fishing boat you see a big liner plowing a steady course. It tells you that the ocean is one of the world's most important highways for travel and commerce.

As you walk along the narrow strip of damp sand at the edge of the water you see pebbles worn smooth by the action of the waves, and thousands and thousands of shells. Some of the shells

are smaller than a penny. Some are larger than saucers. They are of many colors — black and white, red and gray, orange and blue. Some are flat, some are curved, and some are curled into spiral shapes. Each of the shells was once the home of a living sea creature. They tell you something about the thousands of different kinds of sea animals called *shellfish*.

You see seaweed, too, that has been washed onto the beach, and it tells you something about the kind of plants that live in the ocean.

At the far end of the beach, just beyond a village of summer cottages, you see a wall of huge stones thrusting itself out into the water. It is called a *breakwater*. Before the wall was built the sand on this part of the beach was being rapidly washed away. Each year the sea came closer and closer to the village houses. The incoming waves now strike against the breakwater, which blunts their destructive force. Now the beach is no longer being worn away.

The sea can build up land, too. You can see how it has done this at the mouth of a small river that empties into the sea a little farther on. Recently the sea washed so much sand up into the river that boats could scarcely move upstream. That's why a big dredge is now at work, digging away at the sea-borne sand, to make a new boat channel.

As you turn around and start back along the beach you see that the strip of wet sand has grown much wider. This tells you that the tide is going out, and reminds you that the tides of the ocean are always either rising or falling. When the tide is rising, each wave comes a little farther inland than the one before. When the tide is falling, or *ebbing*, the waves are not coming as far onto the beach as they did a few hours earlier.

Now, on the wet sand that was covered by water only a short while ago, you see more shells. Some of them are still being used as homes for small sea animals. Clinging to a rock, for example, is a pair of dark blue, tightly-shut mussel shells that protects the mussel inside from the drying air. These shells, which will not open again until the tide comes in once more and covers them, tell you something about the particular group of shellfish whose members each have a pair of shells. They are called *bivalves*.

Now, too, on rocks uncovered by the ebbing tide, you see one-shelled sea animals — snails and barnacles, for example. You try to pull a barnacle from a rock and find that you cannot move it. This tells you how these small animals live, clinging tight to a rock or the underside of a boat or some other surface that is covered by water at least part of every day.

Here and there, in hollows in the sand or among a pile of rocks, the ebbing tide has left pools of water. The little creatures in these pools — tiny crabs and minnows, perhaps a baby shrimp or two —

12

tell you still more about the animals that make their home in the ocean.

Presently the sea gulls come inland and hover above the beach, searching for food among the sea animals uncovered by the ebbing tide. One picks up a clam in its beak, carries it high into the air, and drops it on a rock to smash it. Then the gull swoops down again, to eat the soft meat inside the broken shell.

Sitting down now on a rock that was underwater when you started your walk, you touch with your finger the thin coating of silvery-white powder that clings to its surface. You taste the powder. It is salt, a substance that in some form or other is necessary to man's diet. This tells you that men can always get salt from the ocean, by letting sea water evaporate and scooping up the powdery stuff it leaves behind. For thousands of years the salt from the ocean was the only kind of salt men knew how to find. Even today, when most salt comes from mines, many people still collect salt from the sea.

13

The rock you are sitting on, which was wet only a short time ago, is now dry. And this tells you one more important thing about the ocean. It tells you that all day, every day, the water on the surface of the sea is evaporating, changing from a liquid into a gas called *water vapor*. When water vapor mixes with the air it makes the air moist. And when air has more moisture than it can hold, it releases some of it in the form of snow or hail or rain. Without the moisture from the sea the earth's plants and animals, and man himself, could not survive.

Slowly you leave the beach. The smell of salt goes with you, and so does the cool breeze blowing in from the water. Your walk along the beach has told you a great deal about the great ocean of the earth.

The Waves

WAVES are caused by the winds that blow across the surface of the ocean. They exist only on the water's surface. Even in a storm the ocean below the first few hundred feet of water is always quiet and peaceful.

You can find out how waves are born by making a simple experiment. Pour water into a bowl until the bowl is filled to the top. Then blow across the surface of the water. Your breath will make ripples that will move away from you over the water toward the far side of the bowl.

Little ripples, like the ones you have just made, can grow into huge waves. But this can never happen in any small body of water. Another experiment with your bowl of water will show why this is so.

Blow at the water once more, very hard, and keep blowing as long as you can. You will see that the ripples will grow higher as your breath pushes longer and more strongly against their backs. They will keep growing as they cross the bowl. They will be highest just before they reach the edge of the bowl and disappear. But not even a powerful electric fan could make the ripples in your bowl grow into real waves, because the bowl does not give them enough room in which to grow. Ripples can grow into big waves only when a strong wind pushes steadily against their backs over a long stretch of water.

Two things, in other words, are necessary for the making of big waves. One is a strong, steady wind. The other is what scientists call a *big fetch*, or a long stretch of open water. Only waves that have a big fetch can travel for a long distance, with the wind at their backs making them bigger all the time. The stronger the wind, and the farther the waves can travel, the bigger the waves will be.

Experts can calculate how big waves will grow, if they know the strength of the wind and the size of the fetch. If wind blows

at the rate of 40 miles per hour, for example, across a bay 10 miles wide, the waves there may grow to the height of seven feet. A 40-mile wind blowing across 800 miles of ocean could raise waves towering 40 feet into the air — waves as high as a four-story house.

Some sailors say that during violent storms they have seen waves that they thought were one hundred feet high. But most scientists believe that waves never — or almost never — get that high. There are two reasons, they say, why even the one hundred-mile winds of powerful hurricanes, or typhoons, probably can not cause waves more than 60 feet high.

One reason is that the very strongest wind usually blows the tops off the very waves it makes, leaving them smaller than those caused by less powerful winds.

The other reason is that hurricane or typhoon winds usually blow first in one direction, and then in another. And when a powerful wind turns around, and blows from the opposite direction, it can flatten out the big waves it has been making.

Giant waves, called *storm waves* or *seas,* do not stop moving across the water even when the wind that caused them finally dies down. But when the wind dies they do change their shape. They flatten out into low mounds of water called *swells.*

Swells may move across the ocean, at the rate of about 15 miles an hour, for thousands of miles. They stop only when they run into land, a strong wind, or big swells from the opposite direction.

When a deep-ocean swell reaches the shallow water near a shore, it changes its shape again. This happens as soon as the bottom, dragging at the lower part of the swell, makes it slow down. Then the upper part of the wave moves ahead of the lower part. The wave, in other words, begins to lean forward, just as you would lean forward if your feet suddenly stuck in heavy mud as you were running across a field.

As the swell leans farther and farther forward, its top stretches out into a thin ridge. And finally that ridge topples forward into a lather of foam. When this happens we say the wave is breaking, and we call it a *breaker*.

A long line of breakers, roaring toward land one after the other, is called a *surf*. A raging surf along a shore is always a sign that not long before, somewhere far out at sea, a wind was blowing that was strong enough to make very large waves.

A raging surf is one of the most destructive forces in the world. It can shatter the strongest pier, or pick up a house and carry it away. It is the power of the surf that builds up and tears down the land along a coast. At certain places along the English coast the surf wears away more than forty feet of land each year. If you bought a farm along that coast, your land might soon be stolen from you by the sea, and you could never get it back.

The Tides

TIME and tide, an old saying tells us, wait for no man.

It means, of course, that time goes by, minute by minute and year by year, in spite of anything a man might do to try to slow it down or speed it up. It also means that no one can change the steady pace of the rising and falling tide.

The two most important things that control the pace of our tides are the movement of the earth around the sun, and the movement of the moon around the earth. The reason no man can change the tides is that no man can change those two movements.

Many centuries ago, when men knew very little about the sun or the moon or the stars, some people believed that the earth was alive. The rising and falling of the tide, they thought, was caused by the breathing of the earth's big body.

Later men began to learn more about the heavens, and this helped them to understand the tides of the earth. They had noticed, for example, that the moon travels a regular path around the earth, and that it seems to rise each day about an hour later than it rose the day before. Since the peak of the high tide also comes about an hour later each day, men realized that the moon and the tide might be connected in some way.

No one understood what that connection was until Isaac Newton worked out his famous theory of the force of gravitation about three hundred years ago. Gravity, Newton said, is the mysterious power, possessed by every object in the universe, to attract or pull toward itself all other objects. The bigger and closer an object is, Newton also said, the more powerful is its gravitational pull.

The pull of the earth's gravity, for example, keeps people — and dogs and houses and everything else — from flying off into space as the earth spins swiftly around.

But gravity can work in two directions at once. Things on the earth, in other words, also feel the pull of the moon's gravitation. The earth feels the pull of the sun's gravitation too, but the sun is so far away that its pull is only half as strong as that of the moon. It is the pull of the moon that is the chief cause of our tides.

As the moon revolves in its orbit, it pulls at the water of our ocean and raises up a part of it. That raised water, like a huge wave, travels across the sea, pulled by the moon, until it approaches a shore. There it moves far up sloping beaches, covers mud flats and marshes, and lifts the water level of bays, inlets, and harbors. It is the rising, or *incoming* tide.

Bay of Fundy at low tide

Tides are not alike all over the world. The water level rises only a few inches during an incoming tide in the Gulf of Mexico, for example. But a high tide in Canada's Bay of Fundy raises the water level 50 feet, giving it the highest tides in the world.

One reason for this great difference, scientists say, is the difference between the size and shape of the two bodies of water. The Gulf of Mexico is very large, with a gently sloping bottom. The Bay of Fundy is a narrow channel between steep walls. A tide flowing into the vast open Gulf can spread out so widely that it doesn't have to pile up very high. A tide flowing into the narrow Bay has no room to spread out, and rises rapidly up the channel's walls.

Not even the most expert scientists can explain everything about the tides of the ocean. No one yet completely understands, for example, why there are two high tides every day along certain

20

shores, and only one every twenty-four hours on other shores.

But by now scientists know so much about the tides that they can calculate the exact hour of the highest peak of the tide at almost any place in the world, on any date in the past or the future. This makes it possible for them to work out, in advance, accurate timetables for the tides. Many newspapers print these timetables every day, because they are useful to so many people.

Fishermen study these tables so that they can be at their fishing grounds when the tide is right for the best catch. Tugboat owners use these tables when they plan their work, so that they will be pulling their heavy loads with the help of the tide, instead of struggling against it. And the captains of huge ocean liners use these tables too, in order to learn the best time to dock their big ships, or to make their way through a channel that is dangerously shallow at low tide.

Bay of Fundy at high tide

Rivers of the Ocean: The Currents

THE OCEAN'S currents are great streams that move in four different ways — *on* the surface, *under* the surface, *upward* like some vast upwelling spring, and *downward* like an enormous slow-moving waterfall.

Scientists still have much to learn about the upward and downward moving currents called *upwellings* and *downflows,* and they have not yet charted all the underwater currents of the ocean. But they do know a great deal about the great surface currents that move through the ocean just as rivers run through the land.

Some of these surface currents are far larger than the mightiest of land rivers. One current that moves across the Pacific from Panama to the Philippines, travels a distance of 9,000 miles. It is more than twice the length of the earth's longest land river, the Nile.

The chief cause of the ocean's surface currents is the broad band of winds that blows around and around the earth at the equator. The eastward spinning of the earth in space causes those winds to blow, always at about the same rate, always toward the west. They are called *trade winds,* because they have been useful to trading ships since the first days of ocean-going vessels.

The main currents, which these winds create, are called *equatorial currents.* They flow westward in two streams, one north of the equator and one south of it.

If there were no land on our globe, the currents set up by the gentle trade winds would move steadily westward around the earth at the equator. But the continents and islands of the world, rising like huge walls in the way of these currents, turn them aside.

South America, for example, stands in the way of the great

westward moving currents of the Atlantic. When those currents meet this wall of land, they are turned aside. One stream turns northward, along the coast of the United States, and travels in a huge clockwise circle around the northern Atlantic. The other turns southward, along the coast of South America, to form a huge circle in the southern Atlantic. This circle moves in the opposite, or counterclockwise direction.

The same thing happens in the Pacific, when the broad currents flowing westward across that body of water run into the continent of Asia.

There are other currents too, such as the Labrador Current, that flow toward the equator from the icy waters around the Poles. And all of these big currents divide into two or more streams when they run into land barriers.

That is why there are, altogether, many surface currents in the ocean. Some are large, some are small. Some are warm, some are cold. Some barely move. Others flow at the rate of several miles an hour, slowing down all ships that try to sail against them, and speeding the ships that travel along with them.

Part of the Atlantic's northern equatorial current, beginning in the Gulf of Mexico, was long ago given its special name, the Gulf Stream. This tremendous current carries a thousand times more water than the Mississippi. It runs northward past Florida and the eastern coast of the United States as far as Cape Hatteras in North Carolina. There it veers to the east, passes Newfoundland, and heads in a great arc across the Atlantic. As it approaches Europe it divides into three streams, one turning north, one turning south, and one aiming toward England.

The water in the Gulf Stream is so warm that it melts icebergs floating southward from the polar regions. It warms the land it

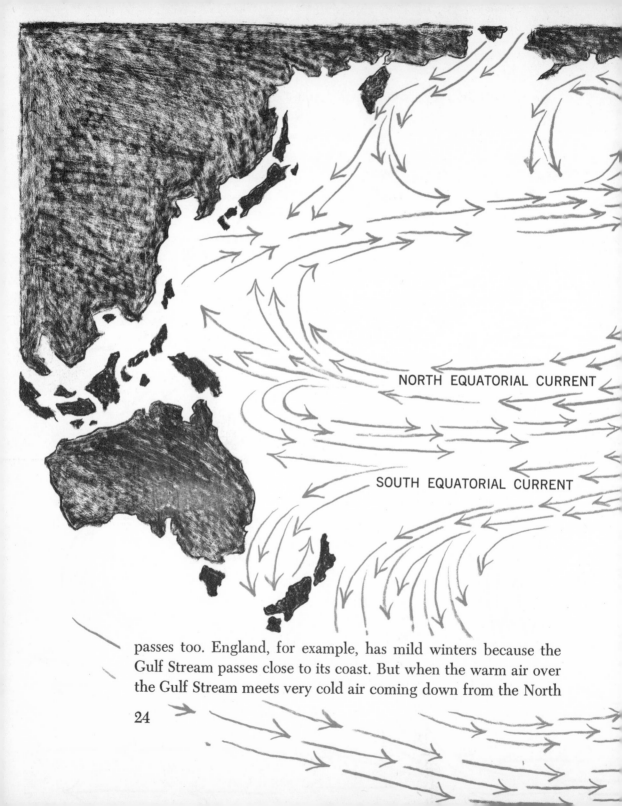

NORTH EQUATORIAL CURRENT

SOUTH EQUATORIAL CURRENT

passes too. England, for example, has mild winters because the Gulf Stream passes close to its coast. But when the warm air over the Gulf Stream meets very cold air coming down from the North

LABRADOR
CURRENT

GULF STREAM

Pole, severe fog occurs. This is why England's climate is so foggy.
Wind, the basic cause of ocean surface currents, also helps to
cause upward-moving streams called *upwellings*. When a strong

An upwelling

wind sweeps aside surface water, a kind of shallow pit is sometimes formed. But even if the wind keeps blowing for days at that same spot, the pit never gets very deep. The reason for this is that water from the bottom of the sea moves upward to replace the water that has been blown away.

Underwater mountains also force deep water to swerve upward, just as an island forces a surface current to swerve aside.

Downflows, the currents flowing downward from the upper level of the ocean toward its depths, are still among the most mysterious of the ocean currents. It is difficult to find them, because they cannot be seen. It is difficult to study them too. But scientists know that a current of water flows downward if it is heavier than the water around it. Cold water, for example, is heavier than warm water. And very salty water is heavier than water that is less salty.

26

A downflow occurs, therefore, when icy water from the arctic region meets the warm water of an equatorial current. The warm water remains on the surface. The icy water sinks beneath it.

A downflow also occurs when very salty water meets water that is less salty. This happens, for example, at the Strait of Gibraltar, the meeting point of the Mediterranean and the Atlantic. Because of the hot sun over the Mediterranean, its water evaporates more rapidly than the water of the Atlantic, and is much saltier. When this saltier water meets the water of the Atlantic, it sinks toward the ocean floor in a downflow.

The fourth kind of ocean currents, the ones that flow along under the surface, are also difficult to find and to study. Four large currents of this kind, for example, were completely unknown un-

A downflow

til the International Geophysical Year, which began in July, 1957. They were discovered then because during that year oceanographers from all over the world were working together to learn more about the depths of the ocean.

One of the currents discovered during that year, in the Atlantic, runs along about 9,000 feet below the Gulf Stream, and in the *opposite* direction to that famous surface current.

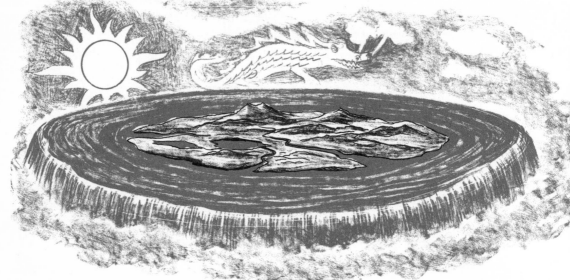

How Big is the Ocean?

LONG AGO, when men believed that the world was flat, they thought the ocean was nothing but a narrow river running around the edge of the disk-shaped earth. The ancient Greeks called that river Okeanos, a name that gives us our word, *ocean.*

The Mediterranean was the only large sea that was well-known to the ancient Greeks, and to the even earlier Egyptians and Phoenicians. All those people lived around its shores. It was the

middle of their world. That is why it came to be called the Mediterranean, which means *middle of the earth.*

Gradually the people who lived around the Mediterranean began to explore lands to the north and east and south. They went north as far as England, south as far as the southern tip of Africa, east as far as India and China. About the year 1271, Marco Polo of Venice traveled overland to the court of the ruler of China, and brought back fabulous tales of the wealth of that land.

Men realized, by Marco Polo's day, that the world was not flat, but rounded like an orange. They also realized that the ocean was not a narrow river, but a great sea that flowed around all the land on earth. But they weren't sure how big the earth was. And they thought the only land on it was the one big area formed by Europe, Asia, and Africa. So they still didn't have a true idea of the real size of the ocean.

Christopher Columbus, for example, had very mistaken ideas about the size of the world and its ocean. Like some other people of his day, he was sure the world measured only about 16,000 miles around at the equator. In other words, he thought the world was only about two-thirds as large as it really is. And he believed that Europe and Asia, together, stretched almost all the way around the globe, leaving a band of water only about 3,000 miles wide between Europe's west shore and the eastern shore of Asia. So he wasn't surprised when he sighted land after sailing westward across the open Atlantic for only 33 days. He was sure he had reached an island of the East Indies. He didn't guess that Asia was still many thousands of miles farther west, beyond the New World he had accidentally discovered.

The first Europeans who sailed across the great stretch of ocean west of the New World were commanded by the Portuguese mariner, Ferdinand Magellan. Magellan himself was killed during the voyage, and only one of his ships returned out of the five that had originally set out. The entire journey took nearly three years. Magellan's men were the first in history to sail around the world, and to have a true idea of the real size of the earth's ocean.

Other explorers followed Magellan, of course. Many of them set out from Europe on a northwest course, hoping to find an ocean route to Asia, shorter than the one Magellan's mariners had charted. A great deal was learned about the ocean by those stubborn searchers for what was called a "Northwest Passage." Still more was learned about the ocean's size when men were finally able to fly above it in planes.

Even today, of course, there are areas near the Poles that have not yet been accurately mapped. But today we do know that the ocean covers more than 136-million square miles of the earth's surface. It is almost 39 times bigger than the whole United States.

Exploring Underwater

IF WE could pump away all the ocean's billions of gallons of water, we could see the spectacular scenery of the ocean floor —

Ferdinand Magellan

undersea valleys broader than the valley of the Mississippi, chasms deeper and wider than the famous Grand Canyon, mountains towering higher than the peak of Mount Everest.

Men have been curious about this mysterious underwater world for centuries. They would have explored it thoroughly many years ago, if human beings could move about in the water as easily as they can move about on land. There are two important reasons why they cannot do this.

First, human beings must have oxygen to breathe. There is plenty of oxygen in water, of course. It is the oxygen in ocean water that keeps fish alive. But fish have a breathing apparatus, called *gills*, which separates the oxygen out of the water. Human beings, who don't have gills, can't take oxygen out of the water. In order to breathe underwater, human beings must take an air supply with them when they go below the surface.

31

Today, the easiest way to do this is to wear the metal oxygen tank called an *aqualung*. Modern skin divers wearing aqualungs have explored many undersea regions, and taken photographs of them too. But if a skin diver goes too deep below the surface, he is in danger of serious injury, even of death.

The second thing that makes it difficult for human beings to explore the ocean's depths is the terrific pressure of the water there.

Pressure is caused by anything that has weight. Even ordinary air, the atmosphere that surrounds the earth like a thick blanket, has weight. If you could cut out a square-inch column of that atmosphere, and put it on a scale, you would discover that it weighed almost 15 pounds. This means that at sea level a weight of almost 15 pounds is pressing against every square inch of your body all the time. You don't feel this pressure because the air in your lungs, and in the other hollow parts of your body, has the same pressure as the atmosphere.

32

But water weighs a great deal more than air. If you dive under only five or six feet of water, you can easily feel its weight pressing against your ears. The deeper you go, the heavier the pressure becomes. Under 200 feet of water the pressure on your body would be about 100 pounds for every square inch.

To keep from being smashed flat by that much pressure, a skin diver's aqualung must supply him with air kept at that *same* 100-pound pressure. Since it is extremely dangerous to breathe air under much higher pressure, the skin diver cannot safely descend more than about 200 feet. Even if he wears a rubber diving suit, and breathes a mixture of oxygen and helium pumped down to him through an air line, he can go down only about 500 feet.

The only way a human being can go even deeper underwater is to protect himself with a metal wall — a wall so strong that it will not collapse even under a pressure of many hundreds of pounds. A diving suit made of metal is one example of this kind of wall.

Other examples are the submarine, the bathysphere, and bathyscaphe. Inside these protective devices a man can breathe air at the normal above-water pressure of 15 pounds per square inch, no matter how great the water pressure is outside. These underwater devices, in other words, make it possible for human beings to explore the real ocean depths.

In 1934, for example, the famous naturalist, Charles William Beebe went down 3,028 feet in a steel sphere he called a bathysphere. This underwater device, fitted with quartz windows, was attached to a long line by which it was lowered into the water and hauled up again. Otis Barton, who worked with him, later went down 4,500 feet in his benthoscope, another kind of metal sphere dangling at the end of a long line.

Still later two French scientists explored far deeper parts of the ocean floor in a bathyscaphe, invented by the Frenchman, Auguste Piccard. The bathyscaphe is a kind of metal-walled, underwater balloon. It is not raised and lowered by a line. Instead it goes freely up or down according to the amount of ballast it carries. In 1954 the bathyscaphe went down two and one-half miles, or 13,287 feet, into the Mediterranean Sea. In 1960 it went down

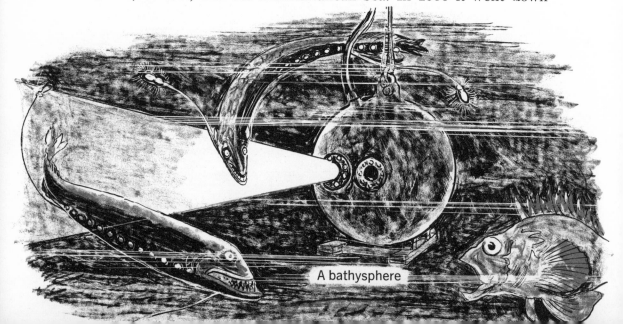

A bathysphere

into the Pacific to a depth of over seven miles, or 37,800 feet.

The bathysphere, the benthoscope and bathyscaphe all have windows through which passengers can see and even take pictures underwater. Underwater pictures have also been made by automatic cameras lowered far under the surface. All these pictures help give us a clearer idea of what the ocean floor looks like.

But in all the world there are still only a few underwater cameras, and very few underwater vehicles like the bathyscaphe. That's why only a very small part of the ocean floor has been photographed. Modern oceanographers say they know less about certain areas of the sea bottom than astronomers know about the surface of the moon.

Fortunately oceanographers can make maps of vast regions of the ocean floor without seeing it, and without even seeing pictures of it. They use the information that is constantly being collected with the help of an instrument called a *fathometer*.

The instrument's name tells us what it does. The first part of the word, fathom, is the name of a unit of measurement six feet long. Sailors measure in fathoms when they take soundings — that is, when they measure the distance from the water's surface to its

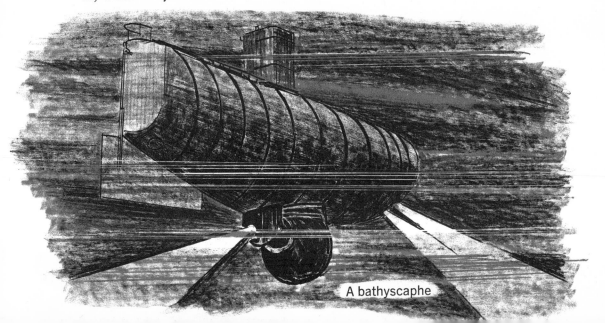

A bathyscaphe

bottom. The second half of the word, meter, comes from the Greek word for measure. A fathometer is an instrument for measuring water depth. It takes soundings automatically.

Mapping the Ocean Floor

IF YOU had a fathometer you could, for example, draw an accurate map of the floor of a swimming pool. You would begin by putting the fathometer aboard a boat, and rowing or paddling over the surface of the pool, measuring the water depth as you went.

Let's say you row first from one end of the pool to the other. The first sounding you take, at the end of the pool, shows a depth of one and a half feet. You could make a record of the measurement like this, in the form of a dotted line drawn downward from a line representing the surface of the pool.

Then, as you row along, you take other soundings, and make a record of them too.

Now, if you connect the ends of your dotted lines, you will have a record of the shape of the pool bottom where your boat passed over it.

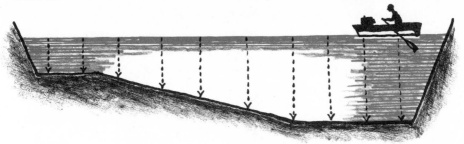

If you make several more trips from one end of the pool to the other, and discover that your dotted lines are alike each time, you will know what the bottom of the pool looks like. You will know, let's say, that at the deep end of the pool there is a level area. You will know that at the edge of that level area the bottom rises sharply, like a steep hill. And you will know that the top of the hill flattens out into a gentle slope that extends to the shallow end of the pool.

There is another method you might use for making a record of the shape of the pool's bottom. You might simply make a drawing, or map, of the pool, and then write down on it the depth of the water at each part. Your map would look like this:

Heaving the lead

Maps of this kind, called *charts*, have been made for centuries and used by ships' captains and boat owners all over the world. A chart shows a seaman where the water is deep enough for his vessel, and where it is so shallow that his ship or boat might run aground.

Of course you could make a chart of the bottom of a pool even if you don't have a fathometer. You could use a rope with a weight at the end of it. By dropping the rope into the water until the weight touched bottom, and then pulling the rope up and measuring the wet part, you would know the depth of the water at that point.

Before the invention of the fathometer, sailors always had to measure depth by this method. The rope they used had a lead weight on the end of it. When they lowered it over the side of a ship, to take a sounding, they called it *heaving the lead*.

A ship's captain ordered his crew to heave the lead when he was guiding his ship into an uncharted harbor, or whenever he thought there was a danger that his ship might run aground. But if a captain knew his ship was in water deep enough for safety, he seldom ordered soundings to be taken. Lowering a rope into the water, and heaving it up again, was a long, dull job. It was done only when necessary.

Even scientists didn't become curious about the shape of the deepest ocean bottom until about 150 years ago. Then, at first, they tried to study it by taking soundings with weighted lines. Their lines grew longer and longer, as they explored deeper and deeper parts of the sea floor. In 1839, for example, a Scottish polar explorer, Sir James Clark Ross, was using a line more than four miles long.

Of course it took many hours to lower such a line into the water, and haul it up again. Often a scientist could take only one sounding in a day. If the sea was rough he sometimes could not lower his line at all.

Scientists soon realized that if they wanted to learn the shape of the whole vast ocean floor, they would need an instrument that could take soundings rapidly and in all kinds of weather.

"Why not send sounds down to the bottom, instead of sending down a weighted line?" some of them suggested. "A sound will travel through water at the rate of 4,000 feet a second. It will keep traveling until it reaches the bottom, and it will then bounce back to the surface as an echo, still traveling at the same rate. So if we send a sound to the bottom of the ocean, and measure the time it takes to get back to the surface again, we will know the depth of the water at that point. If a sound travels to the bottom and back in one second, for example, we will know it has traveled 4,000 feet — 2,000 feet down and 2,000 feet back. This will tell us that the bottom of the sea, at that point, is 2,000 feet below the surface."

The result of this suggestion was the fathometer, which sends sounds down through the water and records the time it takes the sounds to return to the surface again.

Today a fathometer can be put aboard a ship and set to take soundings continuously during a whole voyage. The instrument also automatically makes a record of the varying depths of the water over which the ship passes. The record is a black line drawn slowly along a moving strip of paper.

If the line on the paper is fairly straight, hour after hour, it means that the ship is passing over a flat underwater plain. If the line goes suddenly and sharply downward, and then just as suddenly and sharply upward again, it means that the ship has passed over a steep-walled underwater canyon. Sometimes the fathometer shows that the sea bottom is rising rapidly toward the surface, and then rapidly falling away again. This means that the ship has passed over an underwater mountain whose tip may come very close to the surface.

When the nuclear-powered submarine, the *Nautilus*, crossed the North Pole under the Arctic icecap, she carried fathometers that operated constantly. One was aimed upward, to measure the distance between the ship and the ice above it. This instrument made it possible to locate patches of open water, called *polynyas*, where it was safe to surface. The submarine's other fathometers operated in the usual way, measuring the distance between the ship and the ocean floor. They gave the first accurate soundings ever taken of many Arctic areas.

Thousands of records have now been made by fathometers attached to passenger ships, freighters, submarines, and other vessels traveling all over the world. The maps drawn by oceanographers, after studying all these records, tell us that there are three different kinds of zones, or areas, under the sea, These areas are called the *continental shelves*, the *continental slopes*, and the *ocean floor*.

The Continental Shelves

A CONTINENTAL shelf is a belt of gradually sloping sea bottom surrounding a continent. It is, in fact, a part of the continent — a part that is now underwater, but which was probably dry land during the Ice Age, when the ocean level was three or four hundred feet lower than it is now. If all the ice in the Arctic eventually melts into water, as some scientists predict, the level of the ocean will rise again almost 200 feet. Then many miles of low-lying coastal land will be added to the water-covered shelf around each continent.

Along some shores the continental shelf is very broad. Along the Arctic coast of Russia, for example, the shelf extends nearly

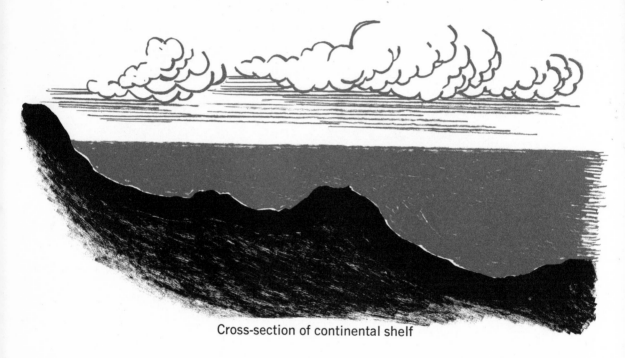

Cross-section of continental shelf

800 miles out from the shoreline. In other parts of the world the shelf is much narrower. Along the Pacific coast of the United States the shelf is less than twenty miles wide.

Most continental shelves are covered by only a very little water close to the shoreline. Some are covered by less than 60 fathoms of water even at their outer edge. Others, for a large part of their width, are covered by as much as several hundred fathoms.

More is known about the continental shelves than about the

other two undersea zones. They are easiest to study because they are the shallowest.

When a sailor of Columbus' day charted a harbor, by taking soundings with a weighted line, he was really mapping one small

Searching for sunken treasure

part of a continental shelf. When a skin diver takes a picture a hundred feet or more underwater, he is usually photographing part of a continental shelf. And it is along these shelves that modern divers go searching for sunken treasure — for the wrecks of ships that went down a month ago, or a few centuries ago, or even as long as two thousand years ago. This kind of ocean treasure hunt, which has taught us so much about the past, also adds to our information about the ocean.

A continental slope, slanting down from
the edge of a continental shelf

The Continental Slopes

A CONTINENTAL slope begins where a continental shelf ends, at
the place where the gradual slant of the sea bottom becomes an
abrupt drop toward the third undersea zone, the true ocean floor.

Some continental slopes are like slanting mountainsides. Others
plunge straight downward like a wall. All are immense. Even the
smallest of these slopes reaches down two or three miles to the

44

ocean floor. The largest one ever charted is a wall five miles high — higher than any cliff on dry land.

There are great gashes in these slopes — huge undersea canyons. Each one tapers downward, like a wedge, from a wide top to a narrow bottom. They are shaped, in other words, like the Grand Canyon. But many of them are much larger than that great gash cut into the earth by the Colorado River.

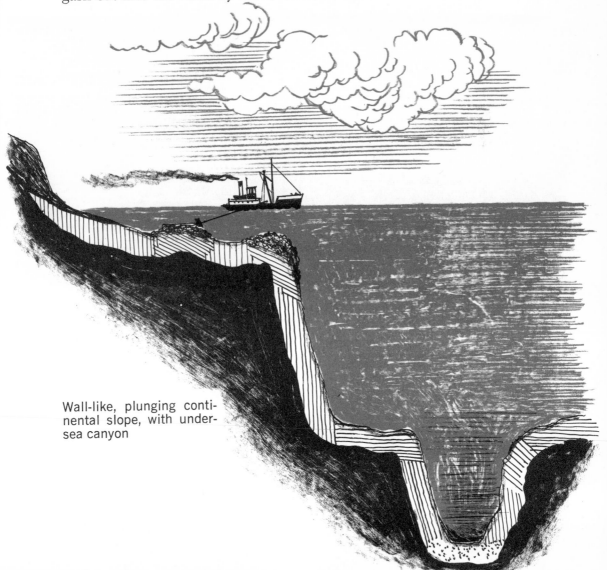

Wall-like, plunging continental slope, with undersea canyon

The Ocean Floor

THE OCEAN floor, the third underwater zone, lies at the foot of the continental slopes and is the true bottom of the ocean.

People once believed that this deep ocean floor was as flat as the flattest plain on dry land. But oceanographers have discovered that only parts of it are flat. Other parts are cut by deep chasms called *trenches*, or they are covered by towering mountains. Some of the mountains are volcanic, and erupt from time to time. The violent disturbance of the water caused by an undersea volcanic eruption produces a huge wavelike movement in the ocean called

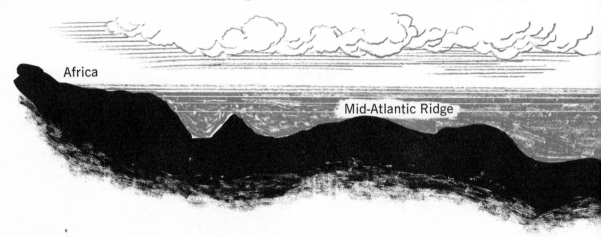

Africa

Mid-Atlantic Ridge

a *seismic wave*. These waves, sometimes mistakenly called tidal waves, can cause terrible damage to harbors and boats.

One of the largest of the many undersea mountain ranges has been named the Mid-Atlantic Ridge. It stretches along the floor of the Atlantic for 10,000 miles, all the way from Iceland to the southern tip of Africa, and even around the Cape of Good Hope. Many of the mountains in this range are as high as 10,000 feet.

The ocean is so deep in the mid-Atlantic that it covers even mountains of that size with a mile or more of water. But a few peaks of the Mid-Atlantic Ridge rise even higher, and poke their heads above the surface to form islands. The Azores, for example, off the coast of Portugal, are the tips of one group of mountains in this range. So are the tiny islands called the Rocks of St. Paul, near the equator.

The thick ice that covers so much of the Arctic hid the shape of the ocean floor there until the historic under-ice trip of the *Nautilus* in 1958. Soundings taken by the submarine's instruments proved that steep, craggy ridges of mountains cross the Arctic

South America

floor too. The *Nautilus* also proved that at the North Pole the ocean floor is approximately 13,410 feet below the surface — much deeper than earlier explorers had believed.

The Pacific has towering mountain ranges, too. The Hawaiian Islands are the tips of volcanic peaks that rise so far above the ocean floor that they break through the surface.

Beneath the Pacific there are also mountains of another kind,

47

A guyot

called *guyots*. Each guyot stands alone, and has a flat top, as if it had been neatly trimmed off with a gigantic knife. Perhaps the guyots once had peaks and lost them. Perhaps they have always had their strange flat tops. No one really knows how they got their odd shape. They are another mystery of the sea.

The ocean's chasms, or *trenches,* are just as mysterious as the guyots. No one is sure, for example, how many there are. But several have already been found and charted, with the aid of the fathometer.

One, five miles deep, is in the Atlantic near Puerto Rico. Another vast trench lies just off the Japanese coast, and there are several near the Aleutian Islands off Alaska. One of the deepest yet charted, called the Mariana Trench, is in the Pacific off the Mariana Islands. This is the trench into which the bathyscaphe dove over seven miles.

Every year millions of tons of earth and stones are carried into the ocean by the world's rivers. Most of this material is deposited fairly close to shore, on the continental shelves and slopes. Very little of it reaches the ocean's deep floor. The carpet of material

48

called *ooze* that covers this lowest underwater zone is made up mostly of tiny bits of shell — the remains of trillions and trillions of dead sea creatures.

These small bits of shell have been drifting down into the sea's depths for millions of years. There they have become mixed with small particles of iron, copper, nickel, and other metals that have fallen on the ocean from outer space, in the form of meteor dust.

To measure the thickness of this layer of ooze scientists set off a depth charge under the surface of the water. The sound of the explosion bounces back to them twice, once from the top of the layer of ooze, once from the bottom. The time between the arrival of the first bouncing echo, and the arrival of the second, tells them how deep the layer is. They have discovered that this sticky carpet of sediment averages about a thousand feet thick in the Pacific, and about 1500 feet thick in the Atlantic.

The top layer of this deep ocean ooze is, of course, the newest. The tiny bits of shell in it are the remains of present-day sea animals. The layer below contains the remains of sea animals that lived many years ago. Layers still farther down contain the remains of creatures that lived thousands of years in the past.

If scientists could study all the many layers in this thick carpet of ooze, they would be able to learn a great deal about ancient life in the sea. They might even discover important facts about the beginning of life on earth, since most scientists think the world's first living things were in the sea, or at the sea's edge.

Someday, scientists hope they will be able to bring to the surface a sample of even the very bottom layer of this strange carpet. Already they have invented a machine, like a giant apple corer, which brings up a round core of ooze seventy feet deep, with all its layers still in place. The bottom layer of this seventy-foot sample is, scientists think, many thousands of years old.

Below this layer of ooze is hard rock — the same hard rock that lies beneath the dry land's carpet of plants and sand and soil. This rock, under the sea and under the dry land, is the earth's real crust.

Scientists have always wanted to drill down through this rock crust so that they could find out exactly what was inside it. But they believed the crust was many miles thick, all over the world, and they thought it would be impossible to break through such an enormous layer of rock. In 1959, however, new sounding devices showed that the crust beneath the ocean, at a spot near Puerto Rico, was unusually thin. Even there it is probably several miles thick, and it lies beneath two miles of ocean water. But scientists immediately began to make plans for sending a drill down through the water and through the rock crust at that place. They even invented a name for the hole they planned to dig. They called it the *Mohole*.

From this strange hole, some day, we may learn secrets that have been hidden since the beginning of time — hidden beneath the earth's crust and the land and ocean that cover it.

Plants That Grow in the Ocean

SOME of the plants that grow in the ocean are so small that they can be seen only through a microscope. Each one of these tiny plants is a single living cell floating freely and invisibly through the water.

Other ocean plants are much larger. These *seaweeds*, as they are usually called, are made up of thousands of cells growing together. Sometimes these groups of cells take the shape of a branching bush or tree. Usually they form flat sheets or long, ribbonlike

Sargasso Sea

streamers. Some ribbonlike seaweeds stretch for hundreds of feet through the sea.

Seaweeds may grow alone as single plants, or in small patches, or in big forests. They may cling to a shallow bottom, or float close to the surface of the water. The most famous floating forest is the one called the Sargasso Sea, north of the equator in the Atlantic. It covers an area as large as the United States. Sailors once feared it, because they believed the floating plants could trap a vessel and hold it fast. Now we know that the tons of seaweed there float about in loose clumps that could not trap even a small ship.

All ocean plants, large or small, growing on the surface or under it, alone or in forests, are alike in two ways.

They all need sunlight. Therefore they all live fairly close to the surface of the water. None of them are farther down than six hun-

A marine landscape

dred feet. Most of them are in the upper two hundred feet of water.

And all ocean plants, large or small, belong to a plant family called *algae*.

Algae, like most land plants, contain chlorophyll. This is the substance that makes it possible for both land and sea plants to use sunlight as power for manufacturing their food out of such chemicals as nitrogen, carbon dioxide and potassium. Land plants take in those chemicals from the soil, through their roots, and from the air through their leaves. Algae, which have no roots or leaves, take in the chemicals they need from the ocean, through their cell walls.

Each cell of an algae manufactures its own food. That is why a small piece torn from a big green sheet of sea lettuce, for example, stays green and fresh. The cells in the small piece go on living, just as they would do if they were still part of the big sheet.

Some seaweeds have tiny air-filled sacs, like little balloons, which keep them floating on top of the water. Some have thin threads or flat disks that cling tightly to stones, shells, boat bottoms and wooden pilings. These threads and disks are called *holdfasts*, and they hold some seaweeds so fast in place that the plants look as if they had taken root. Seaweeds clinging tight to the bottom of a boat are sometimes a great nuisance to boat owners.

One brown seaweed, which has both holdfasts and air sacs, is called the *oyster thief* because it steals oysters from their beds. It has so much air in its little sacs that, when it fastens itself to an oyster's shell, it can lift the shellfish right off the bottom and drift away with it .

Some seaweeds are very useful to man, because they contain so many chemicals. There is a rich supply of chemicals, for example, in the brown and green plants called *kelp.* Along the coasts of Ireland and Scotland, and in many other parts of the world, kelp grows in thick patches on shallow sea bottoms. Men harvest these underwater forests, spread the plants out to dry, and then burn them. From the ash of the kelp they get potassium sulphate, potassium chloride, and other valuable chemicals.

The most useful sea plants — to ocean life, as well as to man eventually — are probably the one-celled algae. These tiny "vegetables of the sea," as they are sometimes called, are rich in minerals, proteins, and vitamins. They form the chief food of many kinds of fish. They may also, some day, be widely used as fertilizer, as a food for land animals, even as a food for human beings.

Algae multiply very rapidly. Experts say they could be planted in huge tanks, and harvested many times a year. One expert says that a single algae farm, covering only about a thousand square miles — an area about the size of little Rhode Island State — could supply nourishing food for the population of the whole world.

Today, in lands where food is scarce, people are already testing algae recipes. They press dried algae into cakes, or grind them into a fine powder and use them in dishes that take the place of meat, eggs, or cheese.

As the world population grows, year by year, and more food is needed, algae may soon become a part of our everyday diet.

Animals That Live in the Ocean

EVERY once in a while on one coast or another, a fisherman finds in his net a creature no one has ever seen before. Experts are called in to study the new discovery. They learn all they can about it and give it a name. Then they add it to the list of animals known to live in the ocean.

That list keeps growing all the time. No one can say how long it would be if it included every one of the animals that makes its home in the sea.

We know already that those animals range from the tiny shell-

TOADFISH

fish called a copepod, no bigger than a pinhead, to the giant blue whale that may weigh close to a hundred tons. We know that they range from the barnacle, which does not move at all, and the snail, which slowly inches its way across the bottom, to the swift marlin that streaks through the water at a speed of fifty miles an hour. We know they range from the graceful porpoise to the awkward horseshoe crab, and from the most brilliantly colored tropical fish to the ugly big-mouthed toadfish.

55

GIANT BLUE WHALE

DOLPHIN

MACKEREL

SWORDFISH

EEL

TUNA

BUTTERFLY FISH

SHARK

LOBSTER

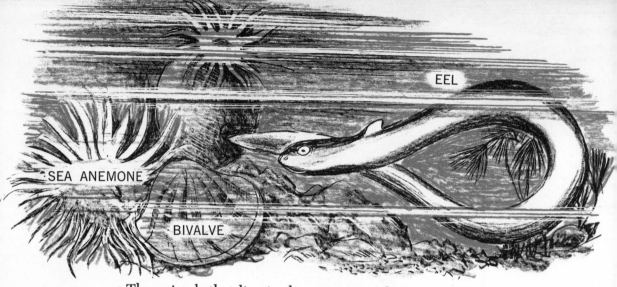

The animals that live in the ocean are of as many different varieties as those that live on land. Each variety has its own habits. Usually each variety inhabits a particular part or area of the ocean.

Some live near the surface, where there is very little pressure and where the water is lit up by the sun. Others live far under the surface, where the pressure is very severe and the water is entirely dark. The light from the sun only faintly illuminates the water at a depth of 1,400 feet. At 1,700 feel below the surface there is no light at all.

Some ocean inhabitants can survive only in warm water. Others die if a current sweeps them away from the icy waters where they make their home. Some live only in very salty water, like that of the Red Sea, for example. Others prefer brackish water, only faintly salty, found where a fresh-water river empties into the ocean.

In other words, the ocean is divided into separate life zones by pressure, light, temperature, and *salinity* or saltiness, and each zone has its own population.

Animals that can live in two different kinds of zones — in both salt water and fresh water — are rare. Eels can do this.

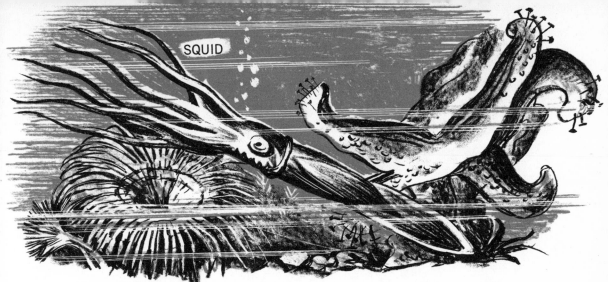

SQUID

Eels are born far out in the salty ocean, but when they are still tiny they make their way toward bays or the mouths of rivers. The young female eels travel on into fresh water, while the males remain where the water is brackish. After several years both males and females swim back to the place where they were born. There their eggs are laid and hatched. Soon the new baby eels set out for the rivers and bays that their parents came from.

The whale can also move back and forth between two different zones. This huge creature is a mammal — not a fish. It does not have gills. Therefore it cannot breathe under water. It must thrust its head above the surface in order to get its air. But when a whale has filled its huge lungs, it can dive more than half a mile down into the ocean, into the black depths where the pressure is tremendous. Then it can shoot up to the surface again, as swiftly as it dove. If a human diver surfaced that fast, even from a two-hundred-foot dive, he would probably die in agony from the dreaded diver's disease known as the *bends*.

Even animals that spend their whole lives in one oceanic zone — near the surface in a warm part of the ocean, for example — usually move about constantly inside that zone in their search for food.

Some sea animals live on plants. The tiny copepod, for example, and other small shellfish live on the very tiny one-celled algae. That is why small sea animals and algae are often found together, in a mixture called *plankton*. Sometimes plankton becomes so thick that it turns acres of the ocean into a kind of "animal-and-vegetable" soup.

The largest animal in the world, the gigantic blue whale, lives on plankton. It swims through a patch of plankton soup with its great mouth wide open. Then it shuts its mouth, squirts out the water, and swallows the tiny plants and animals that have been caught on the rows of bristles lining its mouth. The whale must gulp many mouthfuls of plankton in a single day in order to satisfy its enormous appetite.

But most of the animals of the ocean live on other animals, smaller or weaker or more helpless than themselves. Herring, for example, live on copepods. Mackerel live on herring. Tuna fish live on mackerel.

When human beings eat tuna fish they are completing a food cycle that begins in the sea with the tiny plants called algae.

The best known ocean animals are those that live in the shallow water above the continental shelves, or in the upper six hundred feet of water above the continental slopes and the deep ocean floor.

Among these are hundreds of different kinds of fish, from the tiny guppy to the big whale shark that may be fifty feet long. Most fish have balloonlike sacs in their bodies, called air bladders or swim bladders, which keep each creature afloat at the water level best suited to its way of life. All fish take in their food through their mouths, though they do not all have teeth. Nor do all fish have eyes! Those that have none find their food, at least in some cases, by their sense of smell. Some fish move by *undulating*, or waving, their whole bodies. Others travel through the water by moving their fins only.

The swordfish carries its own bony weapon on the front of its head. The porcupine fish has an armor of bristling spines. The little sea horse, about three inches long, is covered with tough bony plates. Other fish, not so well equipped to fight off their enemies, are protected by a kind of camouflage. Certain striped fish, for example, become almost invisible if they remain motionless among a stand of ribbonlike seaweed. Many fish are white on bottom and dark on top, to help make them invisible to enemies either above or below them.

But fish are only one group of the inhabitants of the sunlit upper waters. Living among them, or in the sand and mud of shallow bottoms, are many varieties of one-shelled animals such as barnacles, two-shelled animals (bivalves) such as clams, crustaceans such as shrimp and lobsters, and odd plantlike creatures such as the sea peach and the sea cucumber.

Each of these animals has its own way of getting the food it needs, of moving about or holding fast to the place it has chosen as a home, and of protecting itself from its enemies.

The pretty little two-shelled scallop opens its shells, takes in water, strains out the tiny plants and animals it can digest, and pumps the water out again. Its method of eating, in other words, is rather like that of the plankton-eating whale. The scallop's shells are also useful when it must move about on the shallow bottom of bays and tidal creeks where it lives. When it snaps its shells shut, and ejects a stream of water, the force of the stream shoots the scallop backward in a kind of jet-propelled leap. The scallop's shells, of course, are also a protection against its enemies.

The single curling shells of snails, whelks, and other similar creatures serve as protective armor, but do not help them move about. A snail or a whelk moves by putting a fleshy sort of foot through its shell opening, and prodding itself along the bottom. Most of these creatures, which move so slowly that they cannot catch living prey, eat the small dead animals they find littering shallow, sandy bottoms. But some of them have tough hard tongues, as rough as a file, which can cut through even a hard oyster shell and reach the soft meat inside.

Some crabs move quickly, in a sort of sideways scuttle. Their speed helps them catch their prey, although crabs as a rule live mostly on bits of dead animals they find on the bottom. The crabs' speed is more important in helping them escape their enemies. Their tough shells are a help too, and so are their two strong, nipping claws. Some types of crabs are very well camouflaged. A sand crab, for instance, motionless on the beach, is almost invisible because it is almost exactly the color of the damp sand itself.

One crab that can move only very slowly is the horseshoe crab. But its shell protects it from many faster animals. Its thin tail, as stiff and pointed as a dagger, gives it the appearance of a pre-historic creature. And that is what it is. This same species of animal existed long before the time of the dinosaurs. It is one of the most ancient animals in the world.

CLAM CRAB WHELK

Starfish are among the most interesting of all the ocean's animals. A dead starfish, lying on the beach, is as hard and stiff as if it were made of clay. But a live starfish can move by means of its flexible pointed arms. Those arms are fitted with many tiny suction cups and they are very powerful. Wrapped around a tightly shut clam or oyster, they can slowly force the shells to open. Then the starfish's stomach, pushed between the opened shells, surrounds the soft meat inside and digests it. Starfish consume so many clams and oysters that they are a menace to the men who make their living gathering those shellfish.

The names of the sea peach and the sea cucumber tell us what these creatures look like. The sea cucumber, a distant relative of the starfish, has a long body quite a lot like a garden-grown cucumber. The sea peach, one of the members of the big sea squirt family, has very much the shape and color and size of a real peach. Like all sea squirts, it has two tubes through which it squirts jets of water when it is in danger.

There are flowerlike animals in the shallow coastal waters too. The best known are the many varieties of the sea anemones, whose small stalklike bodies are crowned with slender, waving tentacles that look like the petals of a flower. A sea anemone is not as delicate as it appears. It can sting and trap almost any small creature that swims within reach of its tentacles.

STARFISH

SEA ANEMONES

SEA CUCUMBER

CORALS

CORALS

SPONGES

One tropical relative of the sea anemone is the coral, no bigger than a pinhead and with a tiny, hard limestone core or skeleton. Thousands of these skeletons sometimes form shapes that look like trees or bushes. Sometimes too, they collect in such numbers that they form great islandlike reefs. The most famous of all coral reefs is the Great Barrier Reef off the coast of Australia. It rises about five hundred feet from the ocean floor to the surface of the water, and it is more than a thousand miles long.

The animals that live in the upper levels of the ocean are well-known partly because they have long been useful to human beings. Men began to learn a great deal about the fish and shellfish of these waters when they started to catch them for food thousands of years ago. And as soon as men discovered the value of sponges and pearl-bearing oysters many hundreds of years ago, they began to dive into the coastal waters in search of those creatures. Divers for pearls, and for the useful animals called sponges, were probably the first men who saw the animals of the ocean moving about alive, many feet under the surface.

Today the animals of the coastal waters are constantly being watched and studied by divers using aqualungs. Many skin divers who took their first dive underwater for fun, or in search of the treasure buried with sunken ships, became so fascinated that they

JELLYFISH

OCEANIC ANGLER

LANTERNFISH

made a career of oceanography, or of *icthyology,* which is the study of fish.

Man's knowledge of the animals that live in the deeper parts of the ocean is still quite scanty. A century ago, in fact, it was widely believed that the cold, dark, lower waters of the sea were entirely empty of life.

But in 1930, when Charles William Beebe made his first deep descent in his bathysphere, he saw living creatures more than 2,000 feet below the surface. Since then, weird dagger-toothed fish, and jellyfish, and squid of strange shapes have been seen and photographed at much deeper levels of the ocean.

An underwater listening device called a *hydrophone* has shown that some of these creatures — and some of the upper-level inhabitants too — make odd noises that sound like drumming, crackling, mewing, shrieking, and moaning.

Many deep-sea animals carry their own lights with them through the dark waters. The lanternfish, which has rows of phosphorescent spots along its sides, looks like a miniature ocean liner with all its portholes illuminated. The oceanic angler has a thread-like line attached to its head, just above the mouth, with a light like a bit of shining bait at the end of it. It swims with its mouth open, ready to snap up any small fish that is attracted to the shining light at the end of its line.

The Ocean in Man's Future

IN THE FUTURE, experts believe, the ocean will supply the world's swiftly-growing population with many of the things it will need — more food, more fresh water for irrigation, more minerals, oil and gas, more power, and more means of transportation.

But before that can happen, a great deal more will have to be learned about the ocean itself, and the plants and animals that live in it.

One thing that must be learned is why fish suddenly disappear from a certain area. Until recently, for example, huge catches of sardines could be made each year off the western coasts of the United States and Mexico. Then, suddenly, the sardines in those Pacific waters disappeared. If scientists can learn where fish go, when they suddenly disappear from a certain region, this knowledge will help increase the world's supply of fish food.

Huge fish farms in the ocean could also some day help supply the world with nutritious food, if more can be learned about the habits of fish. It is already known, for example, that a single cod-fish may lay as many as 9 million eggs, but that only a few of those eggs ever develop into full-grown fish. If scientists can discover a way to preserve all the eggs a codfish lays, this will add many millions of pounds each year to the world's food supply.

Our food supply could be still further increased if ocean water could be used to irrigate the desert areas of the earth. Only fresh water is useful for irrigation, of course, and it has long been possible to make sea water fresh by removing the salt from it. But until recently the methods for doing this were very slow and costly. Now new methods, both quick and cheap, are being tested. If these methods prove successful, vast amounts of water from the ocean may some day be pumped inland to transform the Sahara and other great deserts into good, rich farm land.

Certain minerals and chemicals are already obtained from sea water. Among them are magnesium, and the bromine that is used in the manufacture of high-test gasoline. But there is gold and silver dissolved in the water of the sea, too, along with about fifty other minerals and chemicals. And solid chunks of cobalt and manganese, as big as oranges, are scattered over certain parts of

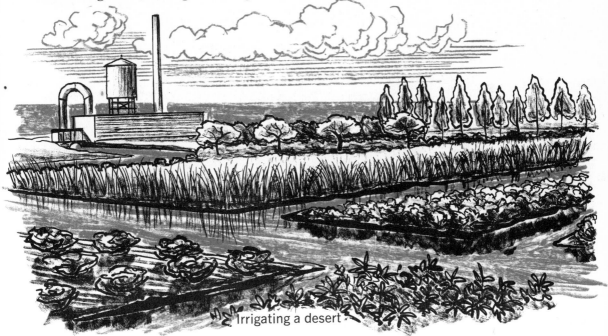

Irrigating a desert

the ocean floor. If scientists can discover methods for obtaining these substances, quickly and cheaply, the ocean will become the biggest and richest "mine" in the world.

Vast resources of natural gas and oil are known to lie beneath the ocean floor. The wells already drilled along certain coasts to-

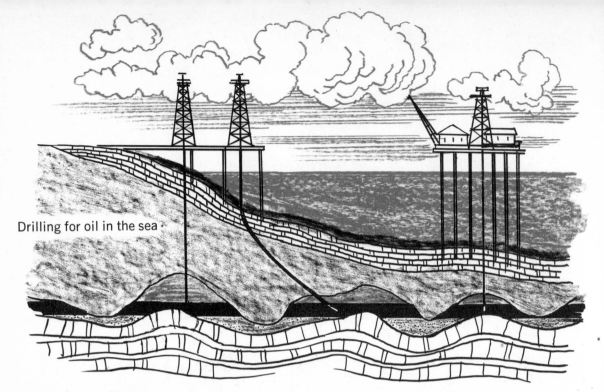

Drilling for oil in the sea

day bring up only a very small part of those natural resources. If scientists can invent methods for drilling oil and gas wells in deep water, they will greatly increase the world's supply of these two products so necessary to modern industry.

Electric power in huge quantities can also be obtained from the ocean, scientists believe, if practical methods can be found to harness the great forces of the ocean's waves, currents, and tides.

The atomic-powered engines of submarines like the *Nautilus* have opened the way, experts think, to a whole new kind of swift, safe underwater transportation. Those engines make it possible for a vessel to travel underwater for thousands of miles, without having to come to the surface at all. This means that these ships can avoid terrible surface storms, and can travel under the polar icecap. The usual voyage by surface ship from London to Tokyo, for example, is more than 11,000 miles long. A voyage between

68

these two cities by submarine, under the Arctic icecap, would be almost 5,000 miles shorter.

Scientists have even designed cargo carriers for the submarine freighters of the future — huge rubber containers, shaped like sausages, which can hold grain, oil, and other products. A row of these sausages, a mile long, holding 12 million gallons of cargo, could be towed to its destination underwater by a single submarine.

Oceanographers are hoping that the atomic submarine may also prove to be the ideal vessel for exploring the ocean floor. If a hull could be built that was strong enough to withstand the terrific pressures far beneath the surface, such a ship could prowl the sea bottom for weeks at a time, making studies that have never been possible before.

Since the days of the ancient Phoenicians, the world's first daring sailors, the ocean has always challenged men to learn its

Submarine freighter of the future

secrets. Today, with the aid of new vessels and new instruments, and with the help of the oceanographers who become more numerous each year, we may at last be close to a solution of the still-unsolved mysteries of the earth's magnificent ocean.

No planet in our solar system except the earth, so far as we know today, possesses an ocean. The reason for this is not yet understood, just as no one yet understands precisely why the earth's ocean exists. But perhaps the space ships of the future, by supplying us with information about worlds other than our own, will help us learn the answer to the greatest of all the ocean's mysteries: why the earth has this vast expanse of water, which makes possible all the life on our planet; and how it came into existence, far in the dim past of the earth's own beginnings.

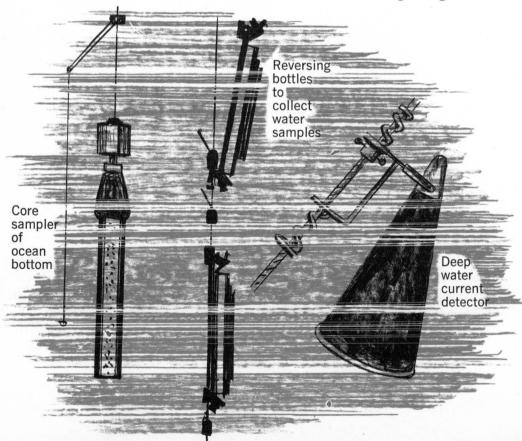

Reversing bottles to collect water samples

Core sampler of ocean bottom

Deep water current detector

Index

72